@fashionandoils

PAIGE SORENSEN

Paige lives in San Diego with her amazing husband and 3 fun children. She owns fashionandoils, and as a professional stylist and essential oil expert, she enjoys helping people discover and project their authentic selves. For speaking or presentations, contact her office. Fashionandoils.com

Follow me @fashionandoils

CONTENTS

"THE WAY WE DRESS AFFECTS THE WAY WE **THINK**, THE WAY WE **FEEL**, THE WAY WE **ACT**, AND THE WAY OTHERS **REACT** TO US."

-JUDITH RASBAND

Introduction

I wrote this book to share with you my thoughts and feelings about fashion and essential oils. I wrote this book to inspire self-discovery and build confidence in you! I wrote this book to help you learn to dress with conviction everyday so that you will feel wonderful and will share your personality fearlessly. I wrote this book to inspire regular people doing regular jobs to remember to have fun expressing who you are through the clothes you wear! I wrote this book for you. I hope you enjoy.

I tend to keep things short and sweet. I am not here to waste your time. I want you to read and learn the basic principles, start implementing them into your life, and then go and do. I will provide specific tools that you can incorporate into your daily routine that will enhance your style and confidence. There will be some fun and interactive exercises in the book, and resources that will help you use these tools efficiently.

I use the words *authentic* and *genuine* throughout the book. Being authentic can be different for each person, but my definition is loving and owning your individuality and being brave enough to show it. I celebrate the differences that encourage us to connect with others in new ways, and to appreciate the brilliance found in the diversity and uniqueness of human beings. Knowing who **YOU** are is the foundation to being genuine and authentic.

I will explain what @fashionandoils is all about and how I merged my two passions, fashion and essential oils, into one consistent business with one powerful message. When there is specific situations described in everyday life, I will add a footnote with recommendations of what essential oils I use for those scenarios. I will also cover some general fashion tips and rules.

My hope is that this book will start you on a journey to help you feel excitement, joy and emotional health while getting to know yourself better. Let's do this together. Please read deeply, with an open heart and mind, and you will learn new things about your authentic self and how to project your message to the world every day. Stay with me, it's good stuff, I promise.

"I just do my own thing."

- Audrey Hepburn

1

I AM A
CLOTHING PIRATE

Fashion runs through my veins. Apparently, I was born this way. I love true, awesome, authentic fashion. Like street fashion and everyday clothing. I am drawn to the way clothing speaks, the way it adds life and character to people. I believe there is so much personal power we gain by clothing ourselves authentically.

When I was a little girl, maybe nine years old, I spent the weekend at my sweet grandmother's house. We ended up going to church together but I hadn't packed any dresses. This is my earliest memory of having that moment of... "Challenge accepted, I've got this! Grandma, show me your closet!" I went shopping in her closet and found a basic, solid grey, hoodless sweatshirt and a brown braided belt. That big sweatshirt went to my knees, I wrapped the belt around my waist twice and tied it, then rolled the sleeves up, and bam! I had created a "look!" On top of that, it made me feel proud that I had created that look all by myself! Yeah, I sported the cutest dress ever to church that day. I remember feeling so delighted that I made something adorable out of a sweatshirt. I was smiling from ear to ear hoping someone would ask me where I got my outfit, so I could eagerly proclaim, "From my mind!"

Years went by and I soon came to realize that I was a clothing pirate. I had a real talent for searching through thrift stores and clearance racks to find fashion treasures—individual pieces of clothing and accessories that I could put together to create incredible, complete outfits but cost next to nothing. I had an eye for style, and a passion to go with it! These moments brought me joy. Pure joy. Over the years, I have perfected and refined these treasure finding skills. If I need or want something, no matter the cost, I will find an affordable version almost every time.

I have a true love for fashion, but not just for myself. That pure joy I felt as a child, I feel often because I discovered that I love providing this experience for other people. My talent for creating fantastic treasures out of someone else's "trash," actually opened my eyes to an even greater strength I had—sharing my talents to help other humans feel wonderful in their own skin. It is pure enjoyment for me to guide others through a process of self-discovery and confidence building, and to teach them how they can be inspired, motivated, and empowered through dressing authentically.

I work with many different clients who instantly become my friends. As a personal stylist, within 5 minutes of knowing you I am sitting in your closet rummaging through your memories and emotions. It's similar to when you hug someone and your bracelet or earring hooks on to them and you are instantly stuck together. That awkward moment of the uncomfortable full body crash, followed by "Whoa, we almost just ruined our outfits!" Then comes the weirdness of frantically unhooking from one another. I just did this the other day and I walked away thinking, "Did I just grab her boob?" Well, I guess we are friends forever now. Once I have stepped foot into a closet we have crossed the threshold of acquaintances and we are now bonded forever. You have opened yourself up to vulnerability.

I have experienced a few vulnerable situations in my life, from silly to scary.

Like…capture the flag in the middle of the night, dressed in all black on a golf course with my older siblings- Wow I was so

vulnerable and scared to death!
Like swallowing a live gold fish on a dare…stupid right?
Like running for Senior class President… and winning!
Like serving an 18-month church mission in Detroit, Michigan.
Like having a miscarriage in a SeaWorld bathroom, yeah, that experience will change anyone.
Like hiring Tiffany Peterson and others to be my personal business mentors. This requires a scary level of vulnerability.

I know some of mine are light hearted. Here are some other vulnerable situations YOU may have faced:

- death of a loved one
- a first date
- applying and getting an interview for a huge job opportunity
- going through a divorce
- adopting a child
- having your first child
- learning a new language
- setting goals and reaching them
- losing weight
- trying out a new hobby
- buying a new article of clothing that is out of your comfort zone

This list could go on forever.

Your closet is probably one of the most vulnerable and intimate places in your home. By allowing me in you are already breaking down a barrier that has been holding you back. This can be your first step into dressing genuinely. I usually consider us fast friends because of this unique situation, coming into your closet. You have invited me into your emotional battlefield. And I come excited! The beauty of this, I have found, is that I help you create a safe place for you to be vulnerable. As we work together, we can identify your individual and unique take on this world. We set on a path to dressing and identifying your true style! It's a wild and eye opening adventure for the both of us. Let's do this together!

Finding My Path

Here is one of my favorite vulnerable experiences that is more applicable for this book. Shortly after I married my stud of a husband we decided to take the leap of faith and do something pretty big! I came to him one day and said, "This cubical desk is slowly killing me, I have to try something different that breathes life and passion into my soul." I know, I am so dramatic, huh? But even at the age of 24, I knew I was destined for more than a cubicle. Well, at that point, I assessed what I was really good at and where my skills and talents were. We decided we were going to open a clothing store. What?! That's crazy as newlyweds! In my mind, I knew I could do it because I loved the thought of working on it every day. Together we took our first big real-life risk and "Paige's Vintage" was born!

We set off on this adventure with a monumental list to accomplish. My husband, Scott, was so incredibly supportive considering he is not a thrifter and quite frankly thinks most thrift stores smell like cat pee. With no money and a big dream, we had a challenging journey ahead of us.

Through my life experiences I've learned true vulnerability leads to real self-awareness. Self-awareness leads to smart calculated decisions. Smart calculated decisions lead to passion-filled execution of true vision. Paige's Vintage was a perfect example of this. Our calculated decision was the beginning of a lot of growth headed my way toward my true vision.

My first task was to find a space for my store with some personality and good energy[*] that reflects me. After shopping around I found a perfect vintage storefront in Sugarhouse, Utah. It had huge windows across the front and side of the store and a large funky door that I painted a bold new color! It was a great location because it was in a college town which had a youthful and eclectic vibe. It was next to a popular local diner so there were people coming and going all the time. Oh, and it was affordable.

Location: check.

Next, I needed supplies to fill my store. Not inventory just yet, but the racks and stuff. Looking back, I now realize that I was exercising the art of abundance. I was thinking and attracting abundance in my life more than I ever had before. For me, attracting abundance is creating positive energy that builds momentum. I say this fully aware that there were snags along the way but with this type of growing momentum, it becomes very natural to problem solve. In fact, being challenged can be fun—pushing through the problems and

---

[*] When I need to add more energy to my day, I use 1 drop of Peppermint & Wild Orange oil in the palm of my hands, then cup my hands over my mouth and nose and breathe in deeply. I like to call this a "human inhaler." After four deep breaths I then rub my hands on the back of my neck.

experiencing the small victories. I was so exhilarated by all that I was attracting into my life. I was positive and determined that I could pull this together and things started finding me.

For example, one day when I was wandering through a mall, actually a mall nowhere near our house so it was random I was even there, I noticed a large clothing store was going out of business. Children of the 80's and 90's do you remember the store Copper Rivet? The main doors weren't closed all the way and without even thinking I carefully shimmied through the gates. I marched my determined butt inside the store wandering through the back until I finally found a supervisor. I bravely asked if I could buy all of the display racks. He said "Sure!" In an instant, and $200 later, I owned all my display furniture, hangers, and shelves. This was a score of a lifetime.

Furniture: check.

At this point I realized in order to fill my store with inventory I needed a small loan. I was in no professional position to get a loan from the bank, so where do you go when you need a loan for a great idea? My parents! I asked my parents and they cheerfully agreed. We had a contract and kept it official of course. Sometimes I wonder if they saw my determination for this idea or just believed in me in general, but knowing my parents and how cool they are, I am sure it was both. After hitting what felt like the $5,000 lottery from my parents, Scott and I went to work. We borrowed his parents SUV and road tripped to San Diego multiple times, searching, shopping, and loading the right vibe of clothing that I thought could sell in that specific college town area. Now keep in mind, this was just before the explosion of Facebook, eBay and Amazon. I am sure some of them existed but they hadn't really caught on to the masses just yet. So most shopping was very limited depending on where you were located in the world.

My vision was to bring a Southern California clothing culture with a twist of clean and current, gently worn clothing to Sugarhouse, Utah. I wanted to provide an environment that had great music, was bright and colorful, full of life, and yes, smelled good! If only I had known about essential oils back then!* I wanted to attract 14-40 year olds to come sift through my discounted, unique, laid back clothing for women and men—which is exactly what I did!

While collecting inventory we happened to hit store after store having crazy discounts. Things like 70% off, or buy one get one free type of deals. It was a miraculous answer to our prayers. I've been shopping my whole life and I've never stumbled on so many bargains like that. Once again abundance was showing up to help me fulfill my vision. Imagine piles and piles of clothes for me to organize. It was so thrilling and scary, similar to when I was a little girl in my grandma's closet, smiling like I owned the world. I seemed to be smiling all the time. We acquired enough inventory with very little money and successfully opened Paige's Vintage a few weeks later.

Grand Opening: check.

But I was thinking bigger than just an average dull used-clothing store on some corner in America. I also featured handmade artisan boutique items that added flair and

---

* My favorite natural aroma is 2-3 drops each of Purify and Wild Orange oil in the diffuser. It is seriously such a fresh, crisp smell and makes me feel happy.

distinctiveness. We had one-of-a-kind homemade scarves and colorful three-dimensional glass stars that were twice the size of a basketball. Those funky stars were a big hit and were made by my creative, artistic sister. This was genius before etsy even existed. We invited local bands in at night, providing them a great concert venue, in a hip underground scene. We always joked that our floor might cave in during concerts. Selling clothes with personality by day, local concerts by night. It was a real thrill!

Paige's Vintage was a success! We were profitable almost instantly. I loved managing it. I loved knowing I created it with my thoughts and actions. I loved knowing I was adding a part of myself and my personality to this pretty cool spot in the world. I hired my first employee, my younger sister. She was the manager and held keys. Sharing these moments with my sisters and family is an incredible feeling. All my sisters, and my parents, would come in and spend hours with me decorating, sorting, organizing, tagging, pricing, designing window displays and signs. The memories of this part of my life are priceless!

I had friends help me mastermind advertising and window marketing. My best friend and I even wrote and voiced a radio commercial together that ran on the air for months. These experiences of creating and birthing an idea and then executing it with the people I love were amazing. Of course my husband was there every step of the way, while holding a full-time job and going to school full-time. Looking back, we were crazy busy living our dream.

Pure Joy: check.

Leading with your strengths and building your life and career around them will greatly benefit you. My store adventure taught me so many valuable lessons. It taught me about relationships and who I can rely on. It taught me that taking time visualizing and planning can dramatically help with execution. Through it all, I discovered a lot about myself! I learned how to navigate the business world. It taught me that

I have killer ideas in my head. It taught me that I am able to visualize a big dream, to see a bigger picture. I learned that I am resourceful, and I am great at seeing what other people are good at, and asking them to help me get the job done. I learned the power of simply asking for what I need. Of course, the answer might be "no," but I found that often the answer is "yes," and all I had to do was ask. I learned that being true to myself helped me achieve my goals. I learned that stepping into unknown territory with confidence does not only change your body language but also lifts your mindset. It also taught me that getting things done is better than ensuring everything is perfect. So many of us want everything to be so perfect that never actually get anything done. Paige's Vintage was far from perfect but successful anyway. One of my favorite quotes ever is "Done is better than perfect."

Since that store experience so many doors have opened. It has presented great opportunities for me that have lead me to my lifelong dream of being a Fashion Stylist. I realized as I was helping people try things on in my store that I had a great eye for styling them from head to toe. I loved watching them walk out of my store more fulfilled and confident then when they came in. Over the past decade I have been able to style and dress hundreds of people and have been able to refine that talent. I love it and I can't wait to dress you! By the end of this book I am hoping you will have a better understanding of how to genuinely dress yourself. This whole clothing store experience was foundational for my future! I draw upon these life lessons daily and am grateful I experienced it so early in my life.

"Style is a way to say who you are without having to speak."

- Rachel Zoe

2

Identify You

Tool #1: Identify YOU

Change can really scare people. But often change goes hand-in-hand with growth, and that's what I see in my job every day. Big changes mean big growth.

After doing some very "scientific" research analyzing my social media accounts and emails, I am prepared to give you the #1 reason why people aren't ready for growth: fear of change.

The most repeated comment I hear goes something like this…

"When I lose 20 pounds I am totally hiring you to makeover my closet."

Stop this talk, now! I mean goals are great, don't get me wrong. But, if nothing else sticks from this book, hear this, truly hear me: You are perfect *now*! You deserve to dress authentically for who you are RIGHT NOW! Stop limiting yourself. You deserve to feel amazing when you walk into every room, every day, no matter what. If those 20 pounds go away, awesome, and good for you. 20 pounds doesn't change your identity though, neither does 50, neither does 5. You are you, so be you now. Don't let that stop you from dressing and showing the world who you are and what you have to offer, today.

The first step to having confidence with what you wear is to Identify YOU!

Tool #1 is **Identify YOU**.

If you haven't done this already, it's time to identify your true genuine self. Let's work on finding the core of who you really are.

Get Out Your Pen!

I want you to remember a time recently when you needed to intentionally dress for an occasion: graduation, date night, wedding, work party, some sort of an event. Now picture in your mind the pressure of pulling together something appropriate to wear. You open your closet to get ready for this event. Say this out loud…

When I open my closet, I am feeling what?

_____

_____

Stop reading!

Seriously!

Answer this question before moving on.

When I open my closet I feel:

_____

_____

I usually hear a wide variety of emotions. Stressed, overwhelmed, annoyed, excited, nervous, disappointed, confused, thrilled and the list goes on.

We all have an internal emotional connection to the clothing sitting in our closet right now. Yes, yes you do. For some, it's a love/hate relationship. For others, maybe you always feel let down. If you don't believe that you have an internal connection to your clothing, then why is your wedding dress still hanging in your closet? Are you planning on wearing it sometime soon? What about that expensive jacket you bought five years ago? Or those shoes your mom gave you? It's a natural occurrence for us to hold on to emotions surrounding the clothes we wear, or just *keep* in our closets. Clothing can and should be sentimental. However, these strong emotions tend to take over our closet, and the line gets blurred for many people. That's where I come in. I am a logical, objective outside voice teaching you what makes sense to hold onto, based on what holds true sentimental value and what does not.

If we have an internal connection to what we own and wear, then naturally there must be an external connection to others when we are wearing these clothes. External connection means how and why people are connecting with us. Clothing is a way that we can connect with each other. It is a significant way to communicate. I don't think I'm breaking news to anyone when I say that most real communication has little to do with words.

Style Survey

To help you identify YOU one of the first things I do as

your personal stylist is conduct a fashion questionnaire. This is where I whip out my "Style Survey". Let's do this together even though I am not there with you right now. I want to be there so just imagine that I am.

These questions, when answered honestly, can help direct you toward a more confident, genuine you. This can minimize unnecessary stress in your life and eliminate the dread that comes each time you open your closet. Imagine how great it would be to throw open your closet with a smile!

Take some time to fill this out. Warning: #1 can be hard but it is so important!

What's your favorite thing about your body? Name 2 things.

_____

_____

What colors are you drawn to?

_____

_____

What colors are you not drawn to?

_____

_____

What image would you like to project to the world? (circle all that apply)

powerful
smart
modest
chic
sexy
put together
down to earth
classy
mature
fun-loving
sporty
relatable
flirty
confident
other:_____

_____

What is your biggest Fashion fear?
(circle all that apply)

being over dressed
not dressing for my shape
not having anything to wear
not matching
not appearing professional
walking in heels
looking ridiculous
lack of confidence
out of style
other:_____

_____

Where do you normally shop?

_____

Where would you like to shop?

_____

What is your most common Fashion emergency?
(circle all that apply)

pants too long/short
armpit stains
static
out of date
stains
not matching
nothing to wear
Camel-toe (talking about leggings)
Other:_____

When you walk into a crowded room, what would you prefer to do?
(circle all that apply)

be in control
blend in
seem natural
be unique
stand out
other:_____

What type of outfits are you looking for?
(circle all that apply)

casual
business
church/worship
services
workout
event

presentation
school
other:_____

Analyzing this survey is one of my favorite things to do! I love watching natural reactions to these questions. My purpose with this survey is to simply identify who you are and how you would like to be received by others. There is value in starting with a strong foundation of self-image and body love. If you don't already have that foundation, now is the time to begin building it. You are an individual and you have an infinite amount of worth!

Understanding the internal connection and the external connection leads to understanding projection, branding and influence. This is usually where I find the disconnect. *Have you ever considered what your influence is on those around you?* We will explore this more in the next chapter.

Finding Inspiration

Fashion designer, Ashley Nell Tipton, is a great example to me of this principle. She understands this internal-external connection really well. Go and look her up. She won Project Runway (which happens to be one of my favorite shows) in 2015 and is the first designer to send plus-size models (or normal sized women) down the runway. When you look at her picture, what do you think? What feelings or emotions do you have? I think she is a fabulous example of drawing you in and making you want to know her more based on what she wears and projects every day. She oozes happiness and creativity. She spreads smiles and color everywhere. She knows her market and her influence is massive. She is a great inspiration to me and is pretty dang good at authentically dressing! When looking at her picture, you can't help but smile. She tends to pull happy emotions out of most people. When I am asked to speak on fashion at events, one exercise I do is show pictures of people to see how the room responds. When I show Ashley's picture it is so fun to watch the room light up. She says nothing but so much is communicated. She conveys a great message with no words, simply based on her style. Being a positive external influence for others can have a real affect on those around you. This is a powerful tool that is significantly under-utilized.

Here are some other celebrity examples that have influence and dress authentically for their personality:

Emma Stone
Dwayne Wade
Jennifer Lawrence
Jimmy Fallon
Emma Watson
Drew Barrymore
Michael Jordan
Chris Pratt
Zoey Deschanel
Janelle Monae

I have thoughts on all of these people and how they strategically dress to project their influence. So many thoughts. Here are a few: Dwayne Wade is known for being one of the most fashionable men in the NBA. His attention to details and execution of a styled outfit is phenomenal. Jennifer Lawrence has a strong confident personality and her fashion matches that perfectly! Jimmy Fallon is a funny smart guy that wants to be invited into your living room. He is fashion forward and a trendsetter. He understands his brand

and his style elevates his humor. Emma Watson knows who she is and is an outspoken celebrity for modesty. Drew Barrymore has done a wonderful job at building her brand based on her personality—feminine and colorful. Michael Jordan's brand is unstoppable. My son wears him everyday and has never even seen him play basketball. Chris Pratt is great at capturing the average guy. He has such a wonderful all-American look and he makes it look effortless. All of these examples are to provide you with visuals of how they have captured their unique personalities through the clothes they wear. Granted, they likely all have stylists that have helped them understand and identify their own style and project that to the world, and it works! The vast majority of us are not celebrities but we too can dress perfectly for who we are. I give you permission to take control over your style. Own it, and love it.

Let's Go Deeper

What I am going to ask you to do next can be hard, but do it anyway. It is needed no matter where you are in your image and clothing journey. I challenge you to stand in front of a mirror and really see yourself. Take some time each day for a week and look at your true self. Find the things you love about your body. Look at your neck, your shoulders, your arms, your legs, your skin. Identify what you love and dress around those. I once had a client say she loves her calves. Fantastic! Let's focus positive energy on wearing skirts or shorts to highlight those great legs. Normally we dress to hide our so-called flaws. No wonder we feel negative emotions when we get dressed. Let's flip this way of thinking upside down. From now on dress to celebrate your assets. Everybody has them, go find yours!

Most of us have received compliments when workin' a great outfit! That feels awesome, right? I am a huge believer in *genuine* compliments. Don't hold these back. It's always a better day when receiving them, so why not make it a better day and give them too. Authentically dressing and genuinely being true to yourself can be hard. Especially when many of us try to live through the lens of social media—meaning others exaggerated, filtered, perfect lives. Let's try to keep this book experience as real as possible.

Who inspires you right now, people you either know or have observed?

_____

_____

What message are they projecting?

_____

_____

Once you have identified yourself, **your** message will begin to flow freely and your influence will become stronger.

Let's Dive Even Deeper - Aromatically Dressing Yourself

What I am about to teach you translates much better if you actually do the exercise with me. Have an open mind and enjoy this vulnerable moment.

What is Aromatically dressing? I am so glad you asked.

First of all, this is where mentors can give you life-changing gifts of wisdom. I did not create this philosophy. I have added my own flair to it, but the core is not originally mine. Vanessa Ovens presented the basics of aromatically dressing on stage at a training I attended. As she went through this process I had chills all over my body! She has taught me and encouraged me how to do this exercise effectively. Her message, which she has graciously allowed me to share here, stirs feelings in me that are difficult to describe. I've learned over time that those are the best kind of feelings.

Aromatically dressing is a practice that has significant depth. It is so much more than the actions and oils involved. Everything about what I am going to share is deeply symbolic, incredibly powerful, and can be one of the most effective tools in identifying who you really are. It will be awkward at first for some of you, and very uncomfortable for others. The reason why is that we are immersed in such superficial stimulation on a minute by minute basis that something this deep may feel very unnatural at the beginning. I encourage you to embrace it and enjoy it.

Before I show you how to aromatically dress, I want to teach you why. I believe our physical bodies are one of the greatest gifts we have from God. We are uniquely shaped, sized, gifted, and challenged. If we view ourselves correctly, it all works together for our good. Regardless of what you see in commercials, in magazines, and on social media, your body is amazing! The tragedy of our technological world is that in order to be ultra-consumers, marketing campaigns are meant to bombard you with messages of what you are *not*. Aromatically dressing allows you to gratefully accept and even come to adore what you are!

Aromatically dressing is a routine that I recommend doing after you shower. Think of the shower as cleaning off the grime and criticisms of the day revealing the vulnerable, powerful, authentic, divine you. This routine will help you stay balanced and give you something to look forward to each day. It has allowed me to meditate and self-evaluate. It has helped me remember my value and purpose. Allow yourself to honor your body and mind and all they have to offer.

Aromatically dressing is such an empowering daily routine that will help you with body image confidence and healing. Morning routines have really helped me to learn and grow and discover who I am and what I want to accomplish each day. Since adding this to my mornings it has had such a wonderful impact on my mindset, my body appreciation, and my overall balance with mind, body and spirit.

Here's what you will need:

- *A small bowl or cup. I use a shot glass with a cute flower on it. I know, right?*

- *Then you need 2-3 Essential oils, I prefer pure therapeutic grade essential oils. My brand of choice is dōTERRA.*

- *Fractionated Coconut oil*

RECIPE
5 drops of each essential oil
10 drops of fractionated coconut oil

I usually use a citrus oil, because citrus oils are natural mood lifters. I also recommend a balancing oil. These usually come from roots and trees, like Frankincense, which promote balancing and calming emotions. Really, just use what brings you joy. Be intuitive about it and you'll be drawn to what you need. It is also important to change or switch up your routine oils so the body can adjust and feel different benefits.

Let's have some fun with it; your attitude will go a long way with this.

You are going to dip your fingers in the oil and rub it on your body, taking time on each body part. The whole process only takes 2-3 minutes. The more you practice the more comfortable you will become.

Experience with Me

Start with your legs. I start at my ankles. Dip in your oils, then rub your legs from bottom to top in big circular motions. Here's the fun part, the secret of this exercise. While doing the motions you will be saying soft, but audible, positive affirmations. For example, I would say something like this, "I am grateful for my strong legs, I am grateful I can exercise and get to where I am going. My legs have taken me on many adventures. My legs help me to be grounded and have strength." My affirmations may not feel authentic to you so please work on your own. Do both legs.

Next move up the body and do your hips. Work that area! Dip and rub. Bring some circulation to this part of your body and continue with the affirmations. "I love my curves and that I have a backside that protects me. I have strong powerful thighs that make me happy."

Next move to your abdomen. This is my favorite part of the exercise. Repeat the same circular motion as you rub your abdomen with oils. I say things like, "I am honored to be a creator. I love my core and all the joy it has brought to my life. I love and appreciate my scars, they prove sacrifice and endurance. I am honored to be a female and to grow life. I adore my stomach." I say these words. It will seem awkward at first, but I challenge you to say it daily and your mindset will change. You will drown out the negative thoughts and images that have been building over time and start to create new strong pathways of positive body image. I promise you this exercise will send messages of love to your heart and your brain will catch on quickly. You will walk with more confidence and live with more passion. It will be freeing.

Next, move to your back. Bend forward and touch as much of your back as you can. Repeat the pattern, stroking from lower spine, upward as high as you can reach. I formulate affirmations about my internal organs and my spine.

Next do your arms, same pattern. Dip and rub. "I love my arms because they symbolize my loving actions toward my kids, my husband, and other people. My arms and hands bring honor to me as I serve."

Next chest/pecks, same pattern. I love to focus on my heart and connecting with my soul.

Finish with your shoulders and neck. I usually say something to the effect of, "I enjoy my neck and strong shoulders and all that they hold. Help me to open my voice and speak freely with everyone I connect with today. "

When you get out of the shower each morning dry off

and take 2 minutes to do this routine. This will dramatically help with being comfortable in your own amazing body and connecting with your inner self. It is quite magical. I would love to hear your experience with this exercise. Please share it with me either by email, or even better, by Instagram. Others need to hear this positive message from as many sources as possible. Will you accept the challenge?

Be sure to hydrate after doing this exercise!*

* I put 1-2 drops Lemon oil in my water daily for natural cleansing and detox. My favorite drink mix is 2 drops of Lemon oil, 3 frozen strawberries, and a sprig of peppermint leaves in a large mason jar with a pink straw! I'm a straw girl.

"One day or day one. you decide."

3

IDENTIFY OPPORTUNITIES

Tool #2: Identifying Opportunities

Let's identify some opportunities you have coming up in the next 3 months that you need to intentionally dress for. What's on your agenda? Do you have any events, parties, churching, presentations, group activities, classes, gala's, trainings, meet-and-greets, date night, girls night, prom, graduation, promotions, concert, celebrations, birthday's, fashion shows, red carpet events? Anything!

Write down 3 please.

#1_____

#2 _____

#3 _____

Now that we have identified events coming up we can dress accordingly. When opening your closet to get dressed for this particular event you now have tool #1 of Identifying you, and tool #2 of Identifying opportunities. Being specific on upcoming events helps prepare you with what to actually wear. The next chapter will help big time too.

Here are some questions to think about when picking an outfit out for a specific occasion.

#1 What is my purpose?

_____

_____

#2 How can I project my personality and message to the room?

_____

_____

#3 How can I be a positive example?

_____

_____

#4 How do I want people to react?

_____

_____

#5 What am I trying to get people to do?

_____

_____

and my personal favorite-
#6 How can I add value to this situation?

_____

Typical 5 year old me, showing my personality.

I work with a lot of *presenters and trainers in the business world. I have noticed that we all spend a lot of time on our content and our message for things like talks, presentations, trainings, youtube videos, speeches, and teaching, but we give little thought on how we are presenting ourselves visually, and what message is being conveyed without words. We spend hours and hours carefully editing slides for our presentation, crafting meaningful questions, but prioritize our physical appearance as an afterthought. This tool has a huge impact on what you are trying to accomplish.

---

* For any kind of public speaking I use Balance Blend and Past Tense blend for calming my nerves and putting me in my best presenter self. I like to roll Past Tense on the bottom my foot. And I put 1 drop of Balance on the inside of my wrist.

Leather

Here's an example. As a freshman in college I was so excited to tackle my freaking awesome schedule of fashion classes. I sat down on my first day in my first fashion class filled with anticipation. I looked up and I was instantly underwhelmed with my professor's outfit. Now, I get it, this is not a normal situation. I had high expectations for this specific professor teaching this specific subject. She walked in wearing an out-dated, frumpy, red suede suit with a mismatched red jacket, red skirt, and red suede knee high boots. So yes, you read that right, head to toe RED! All around she looked disheveled and stiff. Now that I put this experience into writing she looked uncomfortable. Maybe I was feeling her pain of being uncomfortable. I'll give her the benefit of the doubt, maybe she had a rough morning. However, she was coming in to meet all her fashion students for the first time to win us over, gain our trust and make connections. Just a little bit more thought and overall execution would have gone a long way.

I remember thinking to myself, "Is this a joke? Am I supposed to learn current forward fashion education from this outdated, unpolished professor?" It created a huge disconnect between her and I. It was one of those moments of immediately wishing I could connect with a teacher who in some way was going to shape my future. One of those moments where I was excited for this new adventure and she dulled my experience. Interestingly enough, through the semester she never really offered much educational value. I know you must think I am so snotty, but this left a real impact on me and I have thought of it often. Let me say this again, clothing and style can have the power to connect or disconnect us with others.

I often have people make awkward comments to me about judging their outfit. Or they think I am constantly breaking down what they are wearing. After that story I am sure you think I do. Nope! I am, however, always looking and observing and enjoying the colors and pieces people pair together for inspiration. But in general, no, I do not judge outfits on a daily basis, unless you hire me. My professor was a different story. My expectation was high.

This example shows that if you are presenting or speaking or trying to connect with an audience concerning a specific message, take some time to think out what you are wearing. Often, when and if we put thought into this, we align our message with our clothing and our message becomes more powerful.

Let me contrast this with another example I experienced recently. I had the privilege of attending a corporate event to hear an amazing, well-known speaker, Carey Lohrenz. She walked out on stage in front of 20,000 people with a huge smile, wearing a black form-fitting leather dress and black knee-high boots. She appeared polished, strong and confident. Oh, and happy! Of course she piqued my interest based on her clothing choice. I think we've already established that it is a risk wearing head-to-toe leather. She proceeded to give the most inspiring message about being the first female F-14 Tomcat pilot for the United States Navy. Her message is powerful and you should look her up. I was so proud of her thoughtful feminine perspective on a historically masculine subject. My point is, her style matched her message. Her message was high speed, edgy, hard-working, determined, confident, unapologetic, pioneering, tough, and courageous. Her clothing enhanced and aligned with all of this. It matched who she was authentically and we, the audience, were able to know her and connect with her instantly. We were invested! By the end, in a sea of thousands, I felt like I knew her personally. This was a much different experience than I had with my professor.

When we don't take the time to plan out our clothing there is usually a reason. I firmly believe the psychology behind this is because you have too many options to pick from (aka your closet is packed full of crap). You have no idea where to start or you act like you just don't care. You need to be crystal clear or intentional about what you are dressing for. Let's intentionally dress ourselves.

" *I can't think of any better representation of beauty than someone who is unafraid to be herself*"

- Emma Stone

4

EXECUTION!

Tool #3 Execution!

Now let's execute! Most people start this entire process backwards. We open the closet to execute with little thought to the situation, and almost no thought regarding identity. No wonder your closet brings out such negative emotions. The reason I usually get hired is because after years of this routine you're extremely frustrated.

This is backwards thinking!

Tool #1	Tool #2	Tool #3
Internal & External Connection	Identify Opportunities	Execution & Influence

Prioritizing tool #3, then tool #2 and then finally tool #1 is wrong. Think about this next time you try to execute an outfit. You probably do this more often than you think. When you recognize you are doing this, take a step back and look in the mirror. We usually don't look in the mirror until the execution process of an outfit. I am challenging you to look in the mirror before and identify yourself, what you want to accomplish, and where you are going. Don't get discouraged, this may sound like it takes a lot of time. Take it from me, the more you train your brain to think about identity first and execution last this will eventually become second nature to you. Execution is the confirmation of a well thought out plan. Tool #1 and tool #2 will make tool #3, execution, simple and enjoyable.

Let's dive right into, HOW do I execute everything I just learned about myself?

Healthy Boundaries

Well, budgeting has a lot to do with this.

What is your monthly clothing budget?

_____

_____

What are you comfortable spending or not spending your money on?

_____

_____

On a scale of 1 to 10, with 10 being high, how much value do you place on what you wear?

_____

_____

I am just going to come right out and say it, I am a minimalist! Or at least a version of a minimalist. No, I don't live in a 200 square foot tiny house, in the middle of the desert, totally off the grid (but I would love that life). But I refuse to be buried by useless junk. I don't think closets need to be packed full to feel like you have options. I fully believe we all have a boundary of how much we are willing to emotionally manage in a healthy way. We are constantly being told to buy more. We don't need to be ultra-consumers to be fashionable. Often buying more and adding more to your closet just piles on more stress and anxiety. An observation I've had is when owning a large amount of things it can cloud, confuse, and stifle your identity with too many options. So many of us get lost in a mountain of things.

I have a couple great examples of this: think of Costco. Don't we all love Costco? I mean everything is better at Costco. The prices, the sizes, the options and the quality. Let's talk options. Costco has done this genius thing for us. They make clear decisions on the front end of what products they carry and then, only offer 2-3 quality options within that category. They have removed the paralysis of options for consumers who have to make decisions while shopping. If you know you need tortillas (which happen to be my favorite product from Costco, the uncooked ones, haha.) they only carry three options. They have eliminated the stress of picking from 20 brands. Thank you Costco! It's so refreshing to shop there because they have already made so many choices for us, unless you are shopping around a holiday which is crazy stressful but for other reasons. By the way, this isn't just my observation, this is a real thing that analysts track.

My second example is a trend within the community and culture of most millionaires. Someone like Steve Jobs who needs to make significant business decisions everyday balances that mental stress by limiting most routine daily decision. Their strategy is to own 20 of the same exact shirts and pants to eliminate those extra decisions in the morning. They have simplified their morning routine by always knowing what to wear. Many CEO's, women and men, do this because they simply don't want to face their closets every day. They have found what works, and trust in that process. It is interesting that Steve Jobs wore such plain clothes while creating revolutionary style in personal electronics.

These examples do not apply to everyone; there is always latitude in the area of execution. Many of us *want* more variety in our style, but avoid the trap of owning too much which ends up clouding our style instead. Personally, I always have a smaller closet but I wear and love everything I own! I know my healthy boundaries for my closet.

What is your healthy boundary? Use numbers—how many pants, shoes, shirts, sweaters, skirts, dresses, etc.

_____

_____

_____

_____

Thinking about your closet as it is right now, which would alleviate stress: adding more clothes or getting rid of clothes?

_____

_____

Take inventory on your life. Many times our experiences dictate the habits of our closet. Let me share with you a few examples of my life that have shaped this healthy boundary for me.

I grew up in the foothills of San Diego. My high school years consisted of going to thrift stores and unique boutiques all around San Diego. The highlight was shopping the best road in southern California, Garnet Ave in Pacific Beach. It would easily take all day to hit the many shops down that road. Whether roaming around or actually looking for different pieces to add to my closet, I was always inspired. Inspired to think outside the marketed box or the average trends of that moment. I drove away exhausted and fulfilled with a new vision of style and fashion.

I also grew up with Horton Plaza which is a 3-story outdoor mall but usually a snooze-fest for tourists. Other options were North County Fair and Parkway Plaza. These were just your average malls with average outfits on display. Fashion Valley mall is high end and expensive in my opinion, but really fun to go and window shop.

Back in the day I worked at a store called The Outhouse at the North County Fair mall. It had a laid-back SoCal vibe. It was owned by No Fear. Remember those shirts with dramatic sayings on them? "2nd place is the first loser." That shirt changed lives! I remember setting goals to be a buyer or seller for Roxy. I always thought those clothing reps seemed cool and laid back. They seemed like they had the perfect job. Now, as I look back I am glad my fashion path didn't take me somewhere like that. I'm an entrepreneur at heart. Overall, like many of you, I had an interesting mix of options to shop while growing up.

My personal favorite was when my mom would bring home huge bags of old business clothes from a co-worker who would pass them on to my three sisters and I. This was like Christmas for me! I would carefully go through every piece of clothing, analyzing how I could adopt it, creatively match it with other pieces, and make it work. I loved that woman's generosity and kindness to always remember us Greer sisters. I will forever pass this little gem of an experience on to others. Her thoughtfulness is the foundation of my very own informal clothing recycling program. I never throw clothes away. Instead, I give them to others. I have donated thousands of dollars worth of clothing in my lifetime specifically to teenage girls. The smiles and gratitude from them are worth way more than boring old chucking them and moving on. In a very real way, clothing equals human connection to me! I always find some way to pass on clothing that I loved. I hope doing this will brighten someone's day like it did mine as a teenager.

Some of my favorite memories are of yard sale shopping with my mom on Saturdays. I had no idea then that this would be some of my earliest training in the skills I would need later in my life and career. It also taught me how to let go of clothing, since I knew I could always find something else perfect for pennies of what the original cost was. If you have never dabbled in thrift store shopping, consider trying it!

All of these experiences have helped me develop my healthy boundaries for my closet. Take inventory on your experiences and habits, and define what kind of healthy boundaries you want to set for your own closet.

You have to know how to navigate your area in the world or the internet when it comes to shopping. Whatever your options are, knowing your price point and what you want are imperative. Knowing these details will help you sort through a lot of distractions out there. This will allow you to execute faster and more efficiently.

One last thing. Please, please, don't go into major debt just to look cool. There are so many alternatives. Hopefully, you've already started to realize that you can do this. Narrow down options, find what you will actually wear that enhances your unique personality, and go for it! And remember, if you need help, I'm here.

"With good basics, you'll have endless options."

5

CLOSET
THERAPY

Closet Therapy

I've been in a lot of closets! I am always so excited to enter a new closet and challenge. I swear this makes me feel alive! I love to walk in and help with reorganizing, cleaning out, and making room for new. Most closets have limited space. This space should be filled with items you LOVE and that make you smile, feel good and that work for you.

If you have anything in your closet that has not been worn in a year, it's time to part ways. Cut ties and donate it, or give it away because now you have room to add something you will enjoy and will really wear. It is therapeutic to let go of old items that weigh you down and add stress. Closet therapy is giving yourself permission to move on and change for the better!

If you physically need someone else to do this, contact me. It's what I am good at and I promise you I will help you feel lighter and freer. It is such a wonderful feeling and refreshing when you are done moving through this process.

Wrestles of Life

After Paige's Vintage we decided to start a family and begin a new phase of life. We sold my first baby—the store, so I could take some time creating my actual babies. My fashion light was still burning and a few years in to growing little humans I decided to try for a job at a very large company doing window merchandising. Okay fine I'll tell you, it was Banana Republic. Which is why BR has a very tender place in my heart.

While working there, as an outlet to my creativity and talents, I would end up staying late into the night dressing and placing mannequins. These gals and guys haunted me! Let me just tell you this is one of the hardest things to accomplish gracefully. Wrestling big heavy bodies with stiff appendages that pop off randomly is incredibly challenging and made me feel ridiculous. There's no way this task should be so hard, right?! Trying to squeeze a mannequin into skinny jeans, while wearing skinny jeans is one of the most frustrating things to accomplish. Driving home on those late nights I felt like a club bouncer who had to break up fights all night. I felt disoriented, usually had crooked crack, and my clothes were all disheveled. I was sweaty, weak and exhausted. They are impossible and yet every store everywhere in the world probably does this twice a month on multiple victims. Mad props to all those mannequin wrestlers out there. I feel your pain.

My point is, even doing what you love and filling your cup of joy, there are moments that are really truly hard and awkward and make you question everything you know to be true within your career. So take my advice... suck it up! Just suck it up and do the crappy jobs and do them well. Have a good laugh and just get it done. There is real, genuine humor in some of the tasks we do in our workplace. Just you and the mannequin know the awkward situations you were in together. Dress and handle that mannequin better than anyone else. Do it so well that you make that mannequin feel like it's a real person! Make me proud.

Back to your closet—on my tips list at the end of the book I mention PLEASE I beg of you, for the love of all that is holy, color coordinate your closet. It will help with every morning decisions. If you wake up and open your closet and you know the weather and/or what events you have that day, being able to narrow it down to the color simplifies your life instantly. I find it easier to navigate then organizing by seasons. It looks beautiful and inviting. I do this in every closet I touch. Take before and after pictures and you will be shocked at the difference. Your whole attitude will change when you can sit back and see the difference. You're welcome.

Take some time to go through everything you own. Take inventory on your feelings and emotions. Then ask yourself these questions:

Have I worn this lately?

Does this make me feel good?

Does this even fit me?

Is this a timeless piece?

Take control of your closet and you will find joy in getting dressed every day. *

---

* Blisters from new shoes? Melaleuca and Frankincense are my best friends. 1-2 drops of both on the sore area. I promise.

6

KIDS
CLOTHING

Kids Clothing

If you are spending more money on a pair of pants for your kids* then on yourself, you have real problems!

The End

---

* The top must-have oil for kids is Lavender! Owies, skin issues, bug bites, tantrums/you name and Lavender can probably make it better.

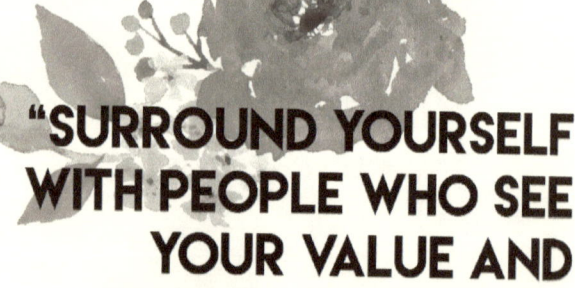

"SURROUND YOURSELF
WITH PEOPLE WHO SEE
YOUR VALUE AND
REMIND YOU OF IT."

7

MENTORING

Mentoring

It is impossible to be where I am without the fantastic influences I have had in my life. Let's talk mentors. Do you have a mentor? I have been blessed throughout my life to always find a mentor to inspire and help me achieve what I am working towards. Many of these mentors I have had to seek out myself. Whether that be a coach for my sports teams, a business mentor, a spiritual mentor, or a friend mentor willing to state the hard realities. My mentors are so different from each other and have all contributed important knowledge that has benefited my life choices. I am a product of the people that I've allowed into my life, and so are you. Who are you surrounding yourself with? People who lift and inspire, or people who diminish and tear down?

A few years ago my husband was really struggling with his occupation. He was good at his job and earned a good income but he was totally unfulfilled. This manifested itself by attacking his confidence. One day, he was sitting in the parking lot of a Taco Bell, feeling totally drained. It was one of those emotionally rock-bottom moments in life. Thankfully, he had already surrounded himself with positive influences. He decided to call one of his best friends and mentors, Kyle. Seconds into their conversation he started to face and articulate his feelings. There's my man, sitting in a Taco Bell parking lot pouring his heart out to a friend that lived 2,500 miles away. After patiently listening, Kyle said something simple that neither my husband nor I will ever forget. He said, "Scott, listen, I've known you for years. Your influence and gifts are amazing. I realize you don't see that right now so please, borrow my confidence in you as long as you need until yours comes back." Those words, from a trusted mentor, eased his pain and gave him a solid enough foundation to find his path again, which he did with Kyle's continuing support. I have since wondered how much longer the road to self-discovery would have taken had he not had mentors who could help him see a clear path at that time.

He raced home to share this beautiful nugget with me. Wow! Such great advice that has stuck with me. If you feel lost, disconnected, small, unworthy, or reduced, imagine me, or someone you know and trust, saying these same words to you face to face:

"Your influence and gifts are amazing. I realize you don't see that right now so, please, borrow my confidence in you as long as you need until yours comes back."

Together, Scott and I decided we needed to rediscover confidence in ourselves, in our marriage, in our relationships, in our business, in our self-images, and in our connection with God. Basically, in every aspect of our lives. From those two sentences resonating with us both, we decided to up level our lives and strive to accomplish more and be true and happy with who we are! We committed to trying harder and building a better life that we actually wanted to live. Don't get me wrong, our life was pretty good before this moment. But we knew we needed to be open to more, we knew we were capable of living more fully, we knew we had more to contribute to the world, we knew we were responsible to have a larger, positive influence.

Bringing "Sexy Back"

Have you ever felt like the universe is speaking to you through Justin Timberlake? Well, it did one day to me, when I decided bringing "sexy back" was my top priority. Not sexy back in the way you are thinking or the way Justin was singing about. Not female/male sex appeal, I mean sexy back into my life, feeling awesome and cool again. Reaching for more dreams! I had to redefine sexy as it pertains to a working mother who still has spunk and life left. Scott and I decided to implement this into our lives so we could focus on adding positive energy and intentionally choosing joy and happiness over feeling tired and over worked. So, we set a plan in motion to bring sexy back and enjoy the life we were building. We said it to each other every day. I am bringing sexy back today! That makes me smile. Try it. Say it loud with confidence!

What career, hobby, or other interests are you passionate about?

_____

_____

_____

_____

What do you want to be better at?

_____

_____

_____

_____

Go and find a mentor today! Go and find someone in your field of interest and take them out to lunch. Call them up and ask them some questions. Pick someone's brain. Reach out to someone who can offer you advice or guidance in that area. Most everyone is willing to help someone out, especially if it's something they have been successful doing. You will find that every successful person needs help from mentors at some point. Most still do! It is imperative that this person be genuinely interested in your well-being. They need to have the motivation to hold you accountable and say hard things when necessary.

Don't shy away from hiring a mentor either. I have done this in the past and it was hugely successful. It will breathe new life into your dream and allow you to be inspired and feel motivated to achieve your goals. Allowing someone in that will help you have a fresh perspective on your options is enlightening and can help lead you to your authentic path.

Books can be a great source of mentoring. I have read many autobiographies that inspire me and teach me new ways to look at things through another's eyes and experiences. I am especially drawn to female autobiographies. I identify with them and watch them push through difficult obstacles in their lives, which is inspiring to me and fuels me to do more and be more!

Love for Learning!

I have always had a love/hate relationship with my educational experience growing up. I graduated High School and did some college and that's as far as I got. Yes, I blame that hideous red suede atrocity my fashion teacher wore the first day. Just kidding!

For many years I have felt almost embarrassed that I don't have a degree of some kind. Why would anyone take me seriously when I don't have a title next to my name? I have wrestled with these questions, and come to find out, as I speak with people all over, so have many of you. Maybe you have had some of the same thoughts I have: Do I really have anything legitimate to offer others? Should I expect success? Can I have any influence on the world without a formal education? I know for a fact many of you feel very similar to me. Especially among those of us who have decided to be mothers as well. In our current culture this can really mess with our identity.

School was an interesting experience for me. Let me give you a quick history. I struggled being in the classroom. It was boring, uninteresting, difficult, and mostly unfulfilling. As you might imagine, I absolutely loved the social aspect of public schools. Seeing, meeting, and socializing with other people and making connections was so thrilling for me. I live my life around the idea that if we're going to do something, there should be a lot of people and we should make it a party! That aspect of school was fun to me!

However, the academic side of it was a real struggle. I had a hard time grasping concepts in the allotted time. I struggled with staying on task and to be quite frank, if it didn't interest me, I was fine not wasting my time. I get a good laugh when I look back at my report cards. They tell a pretty good story. Every single one had wonderful kind remarks from my teachers. Typically they went something like this, "she is such a joy to have in my class." or, "Although she struggles with the work, she's the light of our room," or, "I'm so glad Paige is in my class. Her personality is so fun." I'm sure it was apparent that I was barely surviving academically, and I'm thankful they still enjoyed my uniqueness. My smile and humor probably pushed a lot of F's to D's.

Typical report Card:

P.E.	A+	Who doesn't love a good PE class?
Speech	A+	My speech teacher was so inspiring
Drama	A+	Loved my drama classes
Leadership	A+	This is why I went to HS everyday
Math	D-	Hated everyday of math…still do
History	D-	Didn't value the past till later
English	D-	Wow, I sucked at writing, mainly

because I write how I speak

(Notice how I started with the good grades first)

Have any of you "earned" an F in 3rd grade math?[*] I have. It is not awesome. It messes with you. In my mind that F told me to give up, to bow out, and that I just wasn't smart enough. I assumed learning just wasn't my thing so I shouldn't engage because I'll never get it. But these grades do not represent me being dumb, or being a lazy student, okay

---

[*] When studying, or my kids have a test at school, we use Peppermint for alertness and to support memory recall. Peppermint offers such powerful aromatic benefits. Oh, how I wish I had it in high school! I just breathe it in or put one drop on my tongue.

maybe a little lazy, they reflect me needing to learn and absorb a different way. I figured it out eventually over time. Thank heavens.

So here's the lesson. Take it from someone who was bored with information to someone who now craves it!

Formal education and learning are NOT the same thing.

Obviously higher learning is to be sought after by many. So many people have found tremendous fulfillment in this world through formal education. I'll let others write about that.

My point is, I don't care how you learn. I care that you love to learn.

If you haven't read a book in the last 6 months, thanks for picking up my book. That's why I love biographies, they teach through real life stories. People who love to learn, regardless of the prescribed path seem to have two things in common: passion and accomplishment!! A love of learning brings joy. Joy manifests itself in action. The truly educated get stuff done! They make real change in their homes, and in their communities. If you love to learn you can't help but to go and do.

I've grown so much since grasping this concept. I am now good at expressing I DO have a thirst for learning, I've always loved it, I just had to find my way of learning to truly progress. I had to discover why and how I learned and how to process new information. I am constantly trying to learn and soak in any new information I come across. I have realized over the last 20 years of my life that learning is fun. It is a quest! I'm sad when I think of the years I spent thinking, "Well, it's just not my path to be a great learner." I am passionate that there are lots of paths to education, we are just exposed in our culture to a few in the mainstream. I live outside those options and now that I am an adult and I have figured some things out about myself, I know how to find those avenues. Don't get down on yourself if you don't fit this very specific mold. Pick yourself up and listen to my experience, go out and find what you love to learn about, find out how you like to absorb information, then go from there. It will flourish and grow and give you confidence that you're not broken. I promise.

It's a beautiful
thing when a career
and a passion come
together

8

@FASHIONANDOILS

@fashionandoils

Simply put, my fashionandoils platform promotes the connection between outward and inward health and well-being. I teach confidence with your own body and with how to use therapeutic essential oils effectively. Fashionandoils focuses on our internal health, especially preventative health (essential oils), and our outward projection of self (fashion). As you can tell, I like to have fun and include everyone.

I believe in having tools that help enhance daily living and utilize things that add value to you. Essential oils are one of these tools for me and my family. I have left tips all over this book of what oils to use and when to use them. Just please, do yourself a favor and use them! They are a fantastic, natural, organic tool that will help support your body in functioning at your very best.

My Journey

My oil journey started a little over five years ago. My son had a significant skin issue that is pretty common. We were in and out of specialists' offices that only offered a steroid cream that was pretty dangerous for his age. We were warned to only use it for two weeks because of the side effects. It never took care of the problem. It was a superficial diagnosis for an internal issue. Sound familiar? One weekend we were at a friend's house for a Super Bowl party and I found myself expressing my powerless feelings as a mother not being able to help my son. I did not understand how we could tackle remarkable things as a human race but we don't have a good option for this specific ailment. My friend, and soon to be mentor Robin, put dōTERRA Lavender essential oil in my hand. This was my first real contact with an essential oil and information to go with it. I had never really noticed or considered oils and never even thought to experience them. She said, "Try this. It will work" We left that night thinking, "Really? After all we have done this little bottle of plant juice will help?" But we were desperate parents, so we did as she said. We applied Lavender every night after bath time. We put 5 drops of Lavender and some lotion in our hands and would rub it down the back of his legs, then put jammies on. We did this consistently. It took three and half weeks to start noticing results, and by four weeks it a disappeared altogether. I remember thinking that it had to be a coincidence. There was no way this Lavender oil worked that well and that fast. Well, it did and it never returned. We realized this was a real lifesaver and a money saver too! It was an answer to many pleading prayers of desperate parents.

Learn what essential oils are and how to use them in the back of the book.

This, of course, grabbed our interest with all the other options oils could help us with. I immediately called my mom and sisters and told them this story. They knew our desperation and were shocked at the simple solution. Oils began to spread through my family, and in situation after situation they continued to prove themselves. We started with physical ailments and moved quickly into emotional ailments as well.

We find great hope and are empowered knowing we have these amazing gifts from the earth right here on our kitchen counter. We now have endless stories from the whole family, and friends, showing the miraculous power these tools offer. The oils are a true gift. I believe these tools need to be in every home, every office, every hospital, and school. It is empowering to have options at my fingertips that help my family's quality of life.

After becoming educated, and experiencing the oils, I saw value in the business and company. After all, we found ourselves sharing the oils with everyone we knew! I started to build my essential oil business. I absorbed everything I could. I would stay up late reading the main educational book about oils, Modern Essentials. I learned what plant each oil comes from, how it is extracted and the best possible way to use them.

I started with small daily ailments every family would run into. We actually don't get sick too often but outside of sickness, there are still many little things you face with kids. I began teaching classes, sharing oils, being trained and training my leaders. I wanted to share with anyone who showed interest. I never approached it with the intention of pushing the oils on anyone. That's what's so great about them—everyone needs them in one way or another. I allowed it to organically grow. I experienced as much as I could and loved furthering my education on this new journey.

So many of my business partners utilize these oils in various different ways. I obviously use them with my fashion business. Others use them with their animals, energy work, chiropractic offices, dental offices, yoga studios, gyms, emotional healing, cleaning businesses, and the list goes on. They are so versatile to implement into your life.

Get some oils in your life. Try them and see the power

of the essential oils. If you need help with that, I'm your girl.

Merger

Two years ago, I was working hard on my daily workflow and tasks for my essential oils business while balancing my fashion business. I was sitting at my desk one day and the most amazing thought came to me, maybe I can somehow merge my two passions together? The core of both businesses focus on healthy emotions. Both businesses center on being in tune with your true self. Both businesses are meant to build true lasting confidence. Maybe I could implement my fashion strengths into my health and wellness lifestyle and business. It appears so obvious and perfect now looking back.

My businesses merged quickly after that initial thought. It instantly flowed so well together that I almost couldn't think fast enough. I suddenly had a new take on growing my business and reaching more people. I had built both businesses from the ground up, and now the merger was flowing and creating new energy and life into my new business: fashionandoils. I had all sorts of thoughts flooding my mind of habits I was doing daily, like pairing my favorite essential oil with my outfit for the day, and I knew I could share and educate others on these ideas. It felt unique and totally authentic to me!

I quickly did some research on websites and stylists I was drawn to. I bought the website fashionandoils.com and email fashionandoils@gmail.com. Anything that would help me share my message with more people. I opened my Instagram account, you guessed it @fashionandoils and started having a blast sharing my daily fashion tips. I built and designed my own website. It took me a solid week to just focus on this task and finish it. From there it was all about sharing my message and helping others. I can now get my message out there to more people on my terms with a website, email and Instagram. While all of these help I find my greatest joy in interacting face-to-face with others. I love the energy of presenting in a room and watching individuals have ah-ha moments. Or having that one on one consultation in your closet. Fashion and oils have changed my life, and they will change yours too.

Then came the hard part, explaining my vision and great idea to others. Some didn't get it and still don't understand what I do. That's okay, no worries. But lots of friends and family instantly took to the idea and have been incredibly supportive. I love not only building and growing my business daily but also I love to see the change in people's body language or smiles, just overall confidence once I have a consultation with them. I believe most people want to be validated and complimented and then guided in the right direction based on credible advice. I love the process of transformation I get to lead people through while incorporating the powerful support of the oils to compliment the difficult emotions and ailments we all feel from time to time. It is very fulfilling for me and I experience joy knowing I am living my authentic self every day.

The reason I am sharing my journey with you is to show you that anyone can do this. The process is the same: know yourself, know your opportunities, and then execute! These three tools will take you far in your closet and far in life!

I love fashion, I love helping people, I love sharing new ideas, I love socializing, I love colorful things, I love organic, natural solutions, I love mentoring and cheering my leaders on, I love speaking to audiences and showing them their true value, I love having options and I love a good product that helps you solve problems. I am proud of what I have built. You can do the same in your own way. With your own vision and experiences.

As you have gathered throughout my book, I choose joy* through my life experiences. I absolutely love what I do. I have been privileged with a lot of interesting life experiences to learn from. I have been given opportunities that have been amazing. I am continually introduced to wonderful people who I connect with and who have a positive effect on me. Through my job I am lifted every day because I surround myself with wonderful people. I connect with people through fashion and oils every day. It's my dream career! To sum up how I feel about my business I have created, "My cup runneth

---

* Grapefruit is one of my personal favorite oils to lift my mood. My body craves it. I usually put 1 drop on the inside of my wrist or add 1 drop to my moisturizer.

over."

Go and find what you are passionate about. What do you love? Go and do that whether it's for business or just for enjoyment. Go and do it!!!!! And do it with a smile.

XOXO Paige

PS: You are beautiful right now in this very moment!

PPS: You are loved!

PPPS: Go and Do!

Rules and Tips

I am more of a free spirit in general. I usually don't follow very specific rules when it comes to fashion. I prefer to just be me and let that play out and not be so structured. But here are a few tips that will help elevate an outfit. Let's take you to the next level.

#1 Please stop wearing nylons/tights with open toed shoes. It devalues the rest of the outfit. Men, your version of this is socks with sandals. No bueno.

#2 Edit yourself before walking out the door. When you have too much going on, it complicates what you are projecting. Example, I once saw a business presenter with a headband with a flower on it, feather earrings, 4 bracelets, 3 necklaces, a scarf, a long sleeve shirt, a short sleeve shirt a vest, a skirt and pointy heels. WAY TOO MUCH GOING ON. Do yourself a favor and edit.

#3 I give you permission to wear color. And wear it loud.

#4 Mix old with new, it keeps things fresh!

#5 Have 1-2 really good sports bra's, and that's it. Simplify your workout clothes.

#6 Stop buying your men expensive ties. There are so many affordable options out there. I promise, hit up Tj Maxx, Ross, DaziUSA, Target, The Rack.

#7 Make a joy list! Write down 10 things that bring joy into your life. 5 free things and 5 that cost money.

I was asked by Doterra to write an article that included 7 Fashion Tips after losing weight. I adore my tips. Hopefully they will help those who has gone through an amazing journey of weight loss. Congratulations on the hard work and the determination! Take these tips to heart and allow them to elevate your confidence and style.

#1 FALL IN LOVE WITH YOUR CLOSET AGAIN-
No matter where you are in your weight loss journey, my #1 recommendation is to color coordinate your closet. Not only will you look forward to opening your closet each morning, it relieves so much stress, pressure, and time in putting outfits together. I tell all my clients, no matter what, let's start with making these choices easier every day.

#2 DEFINE YOUR STYLE-
As your body changes you need to honestly and patiently define your style. Be observant and look around. Notice colors, styles and people. What are you drawn to? What do you want to project to the world every day? Try not to get stuck because a lot of these decisions evolve throughout a weight loss journey.

#3 DON'T UNDERESTIMATE YOUR UNDIES
Don't forget about undergarments! In my experience, at least 80% of women are wearing the wrong sized undergarments. This can add extra material, lumps, and bumps in all the wrong places. Pay attention to what you put on first- it's the foundation of all great outfits.

#4 YOU'VE LOST WEIGHT, LET YOUR CLOTHES

LOSE WEIGHT TOO

Let go of the baggy clothes. Fashion is evolutionary, it changes and flows. Allow your clothing to change with you. Give yourself permission to dress your new silhouette.

#5 ACCESSORIES ARE A ONE-SIZE FITS ALL

No matter what body type accessories always fit! A funky purse, scarf, or shoes will brighten your day. Belts are a powerful tool to owning your new body. Jewelry is a fantastic reward for losing weight. Using accessories is a fun way to show your personality.

#6 CELEBRATE YOUR ASSETS, DON'T MAGNIFY YOUR "FLAWS"

I challenge you to stand in front of a mirror and really see yourself. Take some time each day and look at your true self. Let's find the things you love about your body. Look at your neck, your shoulders, your arms, your legs. Help identify what you love and dress around those. Let's flip this way of thinking upside down. Normally we dress to hide our so-called flaws. Now let's dress to celebrate our assets. Everybody has them, go find yours!

#7 BONUS TIP JUST FOR MEN

Invest in slim fit dress shirts. No need to have extra annoying bulk in your dress clothes. It's not just about the neck and the sleeve sizing anymore. Men's shirts include fits like classic, regular, fitted, slim, and ultra slim. Throw the classic and regular fits away. Slim or fitted dress shirts make all the difference!

Essential Oil Basics

What is an essential oil? You ask another favorite question!

You may not have any idea what an essential oil is, or you may have outdated or incorrect information. I will briefly explain what essential oils are, why and how to use them, and the physical and emotional benefits they offer you and your family.

Essential oils are aromatic chemical compounds that are found in flowers, roots, bark, stems, seeds, or other parts of a plant. They are unique to each plant and provide protection from environmental threats, assist in pollination, and often act as the plant's immune system. When you smell a rose, or drive by an orange grove it is apparent these can be very potent and smell amazing. One of my favorite places in the world are the majestic orange groves I live by. The aroma when driving by at the peak of the growing season is powerful and therapeutic. My mood is always elevated.

The unique chemical composition of these plant oils provides a variety of benefits to our physical and emotional makeup. In fact, one drop of pure peppermint essential oil is equivalent to drinking over 25 cups of herbal peppermint tea. Most medications we take have 1 or 2 active ingredients providing 1 or 2 specific benefits. Most essential oils have many active ingredients that provide many additional benefits. For example, pure simple lemon oil is an overall cleansing agent. That means you can use it to clean your counters in your home and also to cleanse your digestive system.

Although you may be new to essential oils, essential oils are not new to humankind. Civilizations have been using them for thousands of years with documented results. There are currently hundreds of studies underway in the United States alone testing and proving the validity of essential oils, many of these studies being done by credible medical universities and research facilities. At https://m.youtube.com/watch?v=31FqzR--KvSs you can see a report on the Vanderbilt University Hospital study that was done, for example. They tested citrus oils diffused in the air (like a humidifier but better) in their emergency room. The result was reduced stress for doctors and other staff members in a very high stress environment. You can also go to the US National Library of Medicine and search for research projects currently underway (www.pubmed.gov). We live in a time where we finally have the research to prove what so many of us have already come to know and experience.

Of course modern medicine has a very important place in our well-being. I have found a wonderful balance of both options for my family. We love and appreciate our advanced medical expertise and all it has to offer us. We also love and appreciate our natural solutions that give us power to protect and manage our daily health.

Essential oils fit perfectly into a healthy lifesyle. They promote clean, beneficial living habits in our daily routines. I have essential oil products in every room of my home. Hand soaps, laundry detergent, cleaning solutions, toothpaste, face wash, lotion, protein shake powder, veggie shake powder, supplements, probiotics, shampoo and conditioner, and so on. All free from chemicals that are proven to contribute to small and large health issues. All infused with essential oils.

Be a User

There are three effective ways to use essential oils. The first is aromatic. I have covered a little of this is a previous chapter Aromatically Dressing. Simply put, inhaling the aroma into your nose or mouth allows these compounds to reach areas within the limbic system in your brain. I always recommend smelling the oil you are using at that moment. This is why diffusers are so genius and effective. They do the job without you having to give it much thought or energy. A diffuser will fill your home or room with the aroma of the oil selected for the specific ailment you are wanting to address. Only put 3-6 drops in your diffuser at a time. I love to mix oils together. One of my favorite recipes is Purify and Wild Orange oil, 3 drops each with freshen and brighten up your home. It's a crisp, clean aroma.

The second way to use them is topically. This is self-explanatory, if you have an issue somewhere on your body, focus the essential oil on that area. My brand, dōTERRA oils, are extremely potent and pure, so use just 1-2 drops more frequently rather than dumping a lot on at once. Be consistent with your application. Also, it is always smart to use a carrier oil like fractionated coconut oil to seal it into the skin and dilute it for sensitive skin. I personally like to spread my oil on my skin so a carrier or a lotion help achieve that. I love using Deep Blue Rub which is oil in a lotion base for easy application. I love using it after a yoga workout. It promotes circulation and pain relief for the areas you strengthened. This is a popular option for athletes.

The third effective way to us essential oils is internally. Now, please know, not all essential oils are created equal. I only speak for my brand of oils, dōTERRA. I know that they are CPTG meaning Certified Pure Therapeutic Grade oils. This means they are put through multiple tests throughout the process of extraction and distillation, assuring that they are pure with nothing synthetic added to them. As such, they are safe to be taken internally, unless specifically noted otherwise on the bottle. I do this in multiple ways. I add 1-2 drops of any citrus oils to my water daily. I add them to recipes when cooking, I put a drop of frankincense or peppermint on my tongue to help with what I am needing at that moment, calming down or a burst of energy. I add 1 drop of 3 different oils to a vegi-cap to make my own concoction to help assist the inside of my body work through ailments. There are many ways to use them internally that can help assist your body.

I feel I must mention, be smart when using oils. Use common sense. Please don't put them in eyes and ears and if your skin feels sensitive dilute that area with anything, coconut oil, olive oil, lotion, but be careful, water can intensify it. We all usually learn this the hard way. On a road-trip a while ago I used peppermint oil and accidentally rubbed my eye afterward. Have you ever felt like your eye was on fire? It's the first time in my life I wished I could accessorize with a pirate patch. Although it was a rookie mistake, within a few minutes the peppermint diluted and all was well again.

I spoke about budgeting with clothing earlier. I also believe the same applies here but with a different perspective. Most of us already buy the products listed above. I'm not asking you to add to your already existing products, I am inviting you to replace them with products that are more natural and beneficial, and less harmful. And you will find that they are just as cost-effective, if not more so, than what you are currently using. Happy oiling!

Oil Tips

Balance Blend and Coconut oil: 2 drops of Balance Blend and coconut oil as an after shave gets the job done.

Balance Blend and Past Tense: For any kind of public speaking I use Balance Blend and Past Tense blend for calming my nerves and putting me in my best presenter self. like to roll Past Tense on the bottom of my foot so no one can smell it, and I put 1 drop of Balance on the inside of my wrist.

Balance Blend and Serenity: If I am needing a restful night, Balance Blend and Serenity blend are my heroes. I put 2 drops of each on the inside of my wrist 30 minutes before bedtime. It's amazing!

Breathe Blend or Eucalyptus oil: are handy to have in my purse or car if I'm battling congestion. I like to rub it all over the tip of my nose so I can breathe it in for a couple hours.

Clary Calm Women's Blend rolled on my lower abdomen for cramping or discomfort really helps! I feel pretty strongly all teenage girls need this in their life.

Correct-X: an ointment with oils in it. It love it on chapped skin areas and under my eyes.

Deep Blue Rub: After a hard workout or yoga routine, Deep

Blue Rub is the best thing to have close by! I Just rub a little on my sore muscles to promote circulation and ease the pain.

Douglas Fir: a great oil for the winter time. It blends well with On Guard in the diffuser.

Fractionated Coconut oil: always a perfect option for blending with any oil for dilution purposes.

Frankincense: my go to oil for scarring. Trust me, be consistent, it pays off.

Grapefruit: Grapefruit is one of my personal favorite oils to help control food cravings and to lift my mood. My body craves it. I usually put 1 drop on the inside of my wrist or add a drop to my moisturizer.

Lavender: The top must-have oil for kids is Lavender! Owies, skin issues, bug bites, tantrums—you name it and Lavender can probably make it better!

Lemon: I put 1-2 drops of Lemon in my water daily for natural cleansing and detox. My favorite drink mix is 2 drops of Lemon oil, 3 frozen strawberries, and a sprig of peppermint leaves in a large mason jar with a pink straw! I am a straw girl. Also, you know those annoying sticky price tags on shoes or mirrors? 2 drops of lemon directly on it, melts it right off. Please take the stickers off the bottom of your heels. It's tacky.

Melaleuca and Frankincense: Blisters from new shoes! Melaleuca and Frankincense are my best friends. 1-2 drops of both on the sore area. I promise.

Peppermint: When I am studying or my kids have a test day at school, we use Peppermint for alertness and to support memory recall. Peppermint offers such powerful aromatic benefits, and how I wish I had it in high school! I just breathe it in, and for a really potent jolt, I put 1 drop on my tongue.

Peppermint Touch Roll-on: I love it! I roll it on my lips and the benefits are minty breath and slight plumping.

Peppermint and Wild Orange: When I need to add more energy to my day, I use 1 drop each of Peppermint and Wild Orange oil in the palm of my hands, then cup my hands over my mouth and nose and breathe in deeply. I like to call this a "human inhaler." After four deep breaths I then rub my hands on the back of my neck—the tingling feeling on my skin is one of my favorite parts of this application.

Purify and Wild Orange: My favorite natural air freshener is 2-3 drops each of Purify and Wild Orange oil in the diffuser. it is seriously such a fresh crisp aroma for my home and it makes me feel happy too!

Ylang Ylang: For extra healthy and shiny hair I always use 2 drops of Ylang Ylang oil half way through blow drying.

Acknowledgements

I want to thank my family for their support and love through this amazing journey. My wonderful supportive husband smiling through all my wild ideas. My adventurous children and the joy they bring to my life.

Thank you to my amazing sister, Coralie Fisher, for the photography and graphic design of the cover and inside of this beautiful book. I am proud of our collaboration together. Designbycoralie.com

Thank you to my editor, Abigail Witherspoon. You helped and supported me in more ways than one. I will always love you!

Thank you, Vanessa Jean Boscarello Ovens, for sharing and teaching me how to Aromatically Dress. Foodalchemy.com.au

Thank you to all my clients for allowing me into your closets and trusting me with your style and reputation.

Thank you, dōTERRA, for sharing these amazing gifts with my family and creating so much abundance in my life.

Thank you to all my friends and family that have loved me for me and have loved my true authentic self. I hope I can return it someday.

Lots of love to you all!

"Done is better than perfect."

www.ingramcontent.com/pod-product-compliance
Lightning Source LLC
Chambersburg PA
CBHW050407290526
45786CB00003B/1169